I Can Be!

Written by
Samantha V. Williams

Illustrated by
Taranggana

I Can Be!

By:
Samantha V. Williams

Contributing authors:
Kayla Williams and Isaiah Williams

Illustrated by:
Taranggana

Copyright: Samantha V. Williams
ISBN: 9798736789245

For you.

I can be anything I want to be,
from A all the way to Z.

I can be an Architect, creating and designing models of buildings and structures before they are built.

I can be a Baker, creating, preparing, baking and selling bread, cakes and other types of baked goods.

I can be a Carpenter, building things such as school desks and chairs using wood.

I can be a Doctor, taking care of people who are sick or injured and advising others how to stay well.

I can be an Electrician, installing and repairing electrical equipment.

I can be a Farmer, growing plants or raising animals for human use.

I can be a Hairdresser, cutting, colouring and styling people's hair.

I can be an Interior Decorator, creating ideas for the design and decoration of the inside of houses and other buildings.

I can be a Jeweller, making, repairing and selling jewellery.

I can be a Karate Instructor, teaching students the martial art of Karate.

I can be a Mechanic, repairing and maintaining machines and engines such as a car.

I can be a Nutritionist, giving advice and preparing meal plans for others to encourage healthy eating.

I can be an Optician, testing people's eyesight, and making and selling glasses and contact lenses.

I can be a **Pilot**, flying aircraft like Aeroplanes and Helicopters.

I can be a Quarry Manager, planning and managing the removal of materials like sand and gravel from quarry sites for use in construction.

I can be a **Realtor**, helping people rent, sell or buy property such as house or land.

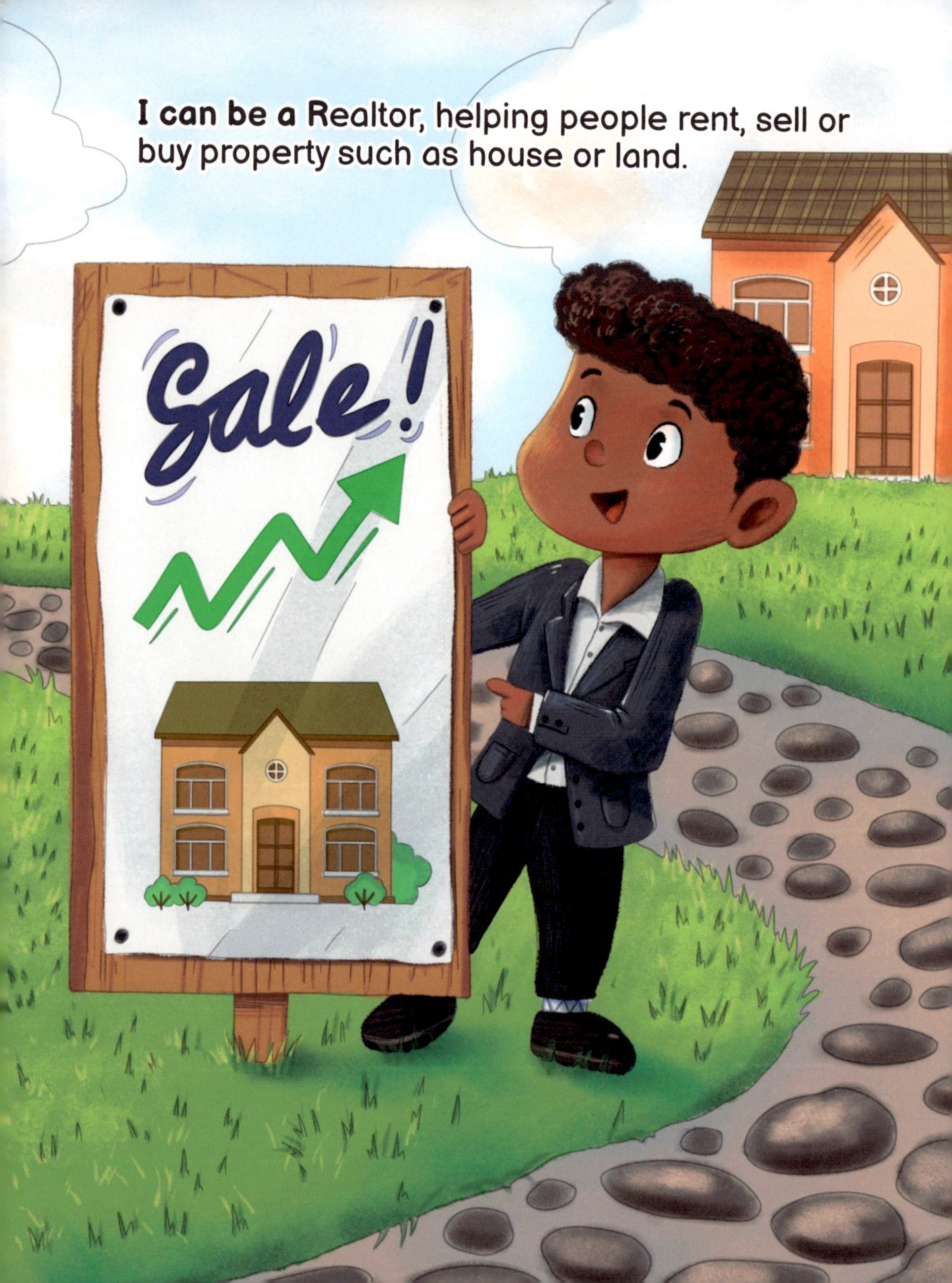

I can be a Sailor, working on a ship or sailing a boat.

I can be a Teacher, instructing students, usually at a school.

I can be an Umpire, making sure the rules of sporting events like cricket are not broken and the game is played fairly.

I can be a Volcanologist, studying the formation and eruptive activity of volcanoes.

I can be a Welder, using special equipment to cut, shape and join metals or other materials.

I can be an X-Ray Technician, using special equipment to take pictures of patients' internal anatomy to help doctors diagnose illnesses, disease or injuries.

I can be a Youth Worker, helping young people solve social, emotional and financial problems.

I can be a Zoologist, studying animals and their behaviour.

I can be anything I want to be, from A all the way to Z.

Samantha V. Williams

About the authors:

Samantha and her children are natives of St. Vincent and the Grenadines. Sam as she is affectionately known holds a BSc (honors) in Youth Development Work, is an Entrepreneur, Mentor, and Co-Founder, and Director of two local charity organizations. Samantha's biggest inspiration is her two children; Kayla an aspiring Marine Biologist and Isaiah who aspires to be a Heavy Machine Operator.

Contact information:

Facebook: Samantha V. Williams

Instagram: samv.williams.2020

Email: sakay273@gmail.com

Other titles by Samantha V. Williams

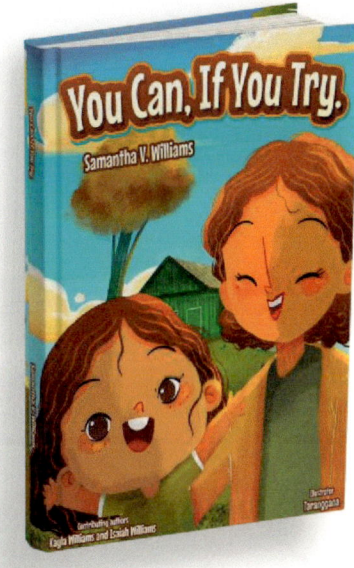

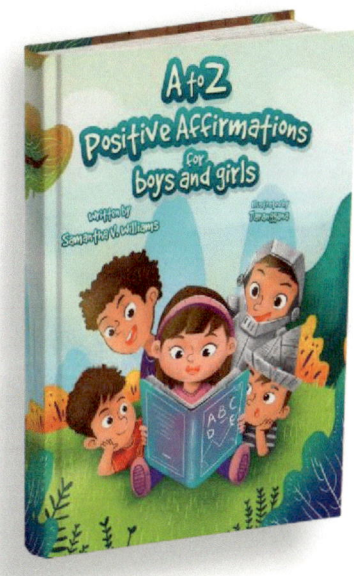

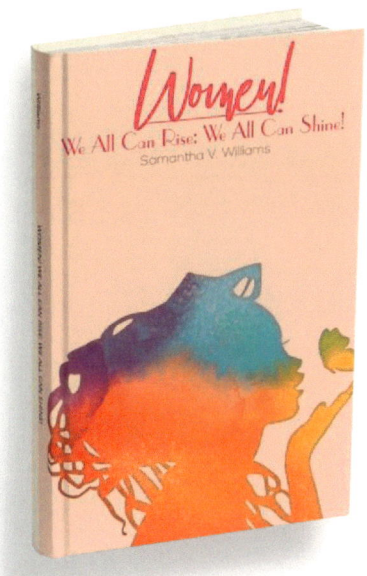

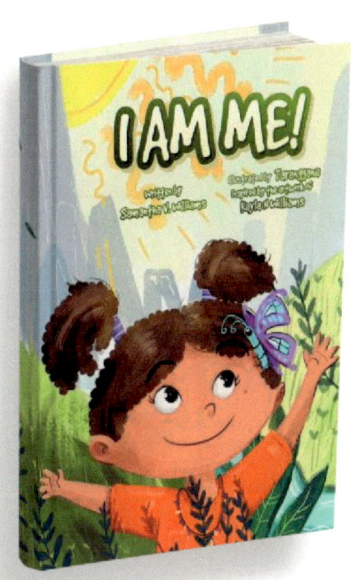

Available locally and on Amazon.com

Made in the USA
Columbia, SC
05 January 2024

29947557R00020